INDIANAPOLIS COLTS

KENNY ABDO

Fly!
An Imprint of Abdo Zoom
abdobooks.com

abdobooks.com

Published by Abdo Zoom, a division of ABDO, P.O. Box 398166, Minneapolis, Minnesota 55439. Copyright © 2022 by Abdo Consulting Group, Inc. International copyrights reserved in all countries. No part of this book may be reproduced in any form without written permission from the publisher. Fly!™ is a trademark and logo of Abdo Zoom.

Printed in the United States of America, North Mankato, Minnesota.
052021
092021

Photo Credits: iStock, Shutterstock PREMIER
Production Contributors: Kenny Abdo, Jennie Forsberg, Grace Hansen
Design Contributors: Candice Keimig, Neil Klinepier

Library of Congress Control Number: 2020919499

Publisher's Cataloging-in-Publication Data

Names: Abdo, Kenny, author.
Title: Indianapolis Colts / by Kenny Abdo
Description: Minneapolis, Minnesota : Abdo Zoom, 2022 | Series: NFL teams |
    Includes online resources and index.
Identifiers: ISBN 9781098224646 (lib. bdg.) | ISBN 9781098225582 (ebook) |
    ISBN 9781098226053 (Read-to-Me ebook)
Subjects: LCSH: Indianapolis Colts (Football team)--Juvenile literature. | Nationa
    Football League—Juvenile literature. | Football teams--Juvenile literature. |
    American football--Juvenile literature. | Professional sports--Juvenile literature.
Classification: DDC 796.33264--dc23

TABLE OF CONTENTS

Indianapolis Colts............. 4

Kick Off...................... 8

Team Recaps.................. 14

Hall of Fame 24

Glossary 30

Online Resources 31

Index 32

INDIANAPOLIS COLTS

For nearly 70 years, the Indianapolis Colts have skillfully bolted past their opponents on the field.

With more than 28 playoff appearances and two **Super Bowl** wins, the Colts leave their fans anything but blue.

KICK OFF

The Colts started out in 1953.
At first, the team was based in
Baltimore, Maryland.

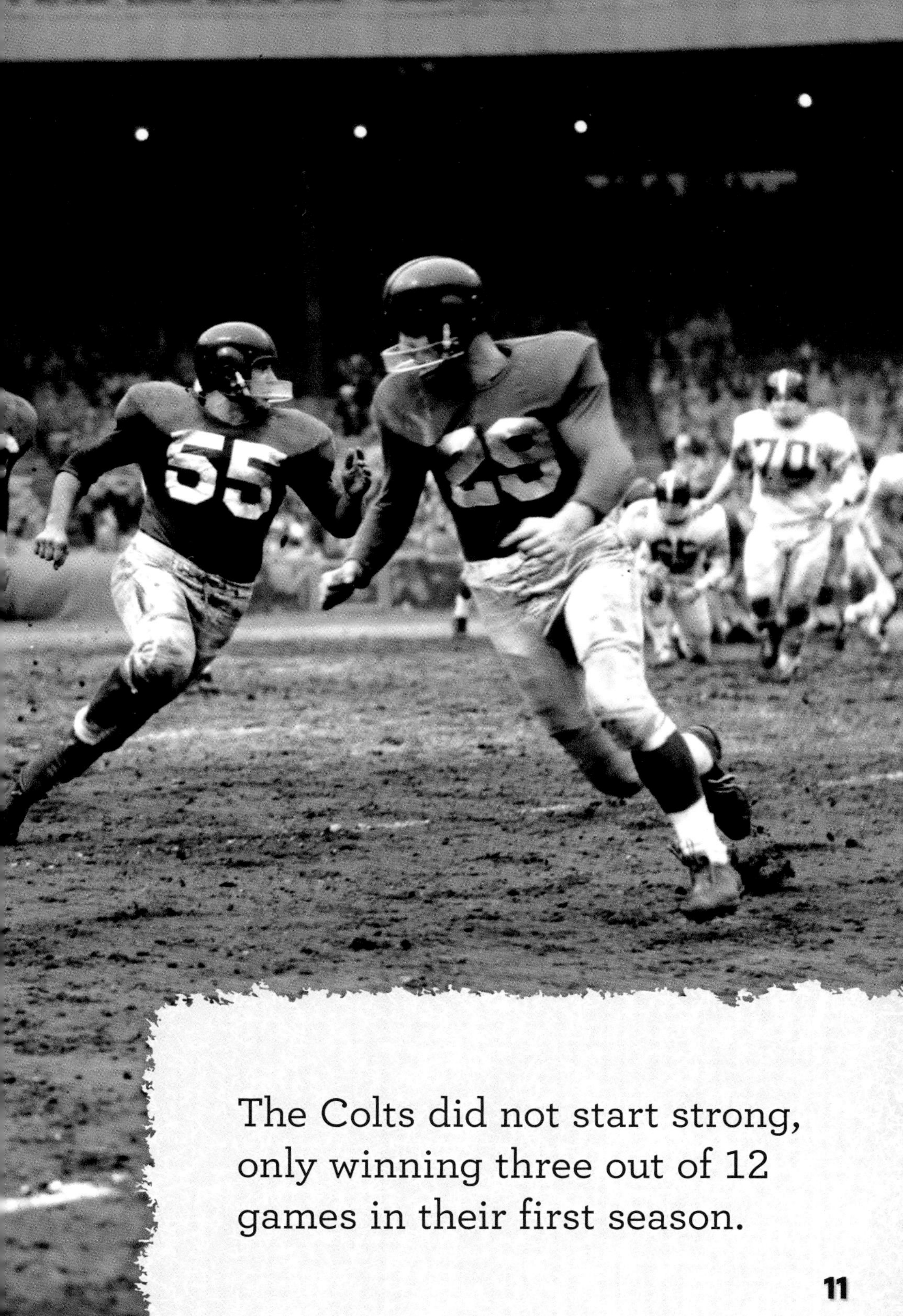

The Colts did not start strong, only winning three out of 12 games in their first season.

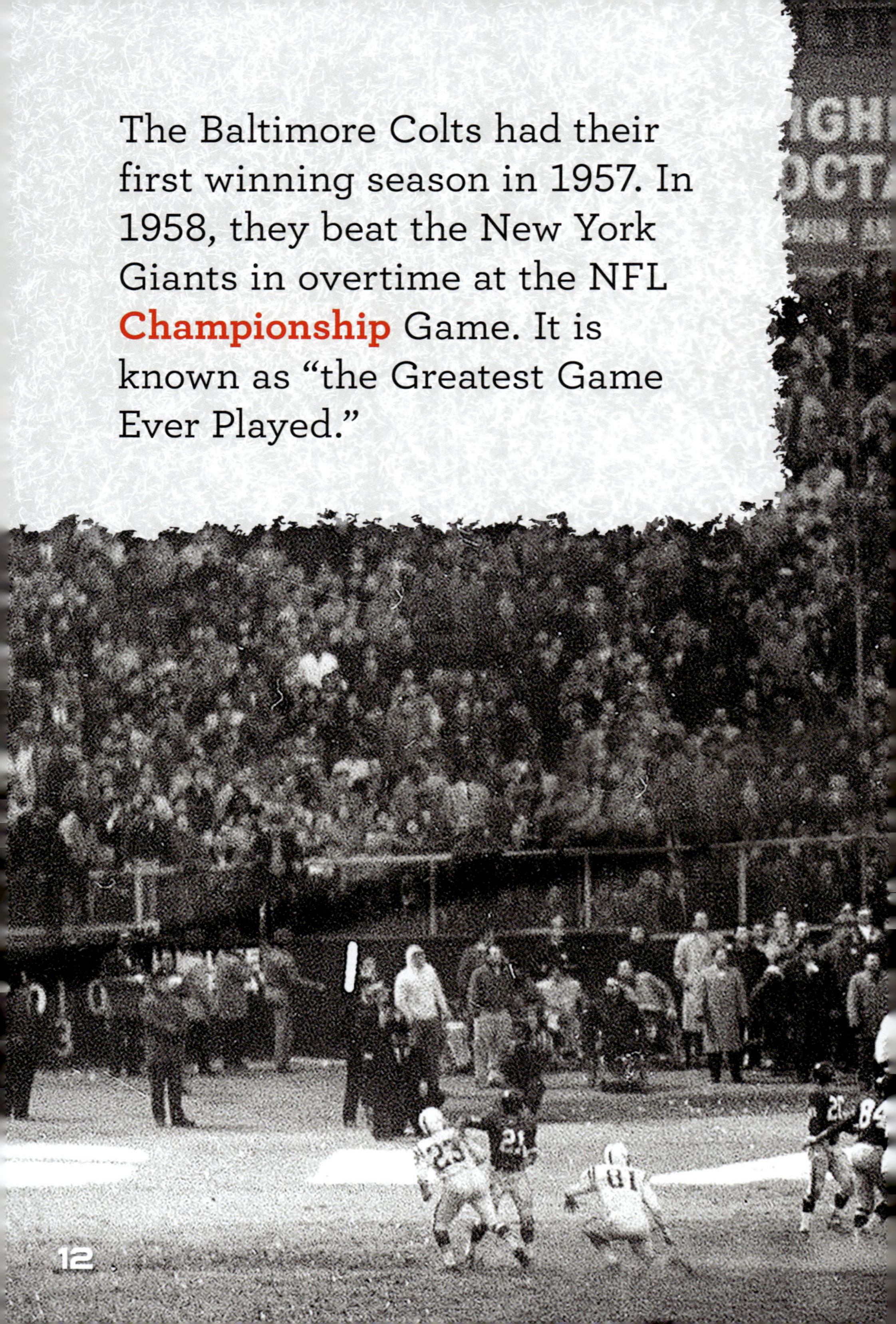

The Baltimore Colts had their first winning season in 1957. In 1958, they beat the New York Giants in overtime at the NFL **Championship** Game. It is known as "the Greatest Game Ever Played."

FLYING A SERVICE
TILDEN

TEAM
RECAPS

The Colts played in their first **Super Bowl** in 1969, losing to the New York Jets 16-7. The Colts made it back to the Super Bowl in 1971. This time they won! They beat the Dallas Cowboys 16–13.

In 1984, owner Jim Irsay moved the Colts to Indianapolis in the middle of the night. For years, the team rarely made the playoffs. But things would turn around after 1998 with a fresh coaching staff and **quarterback** Peyton Manning.

The Colts were back in the **Super Bowl** in 2007. They beat the Chicago Bears 29–17! The Colts went to another Super Bowl in 2010. But they lost to the New Orleans Saints 31–17.

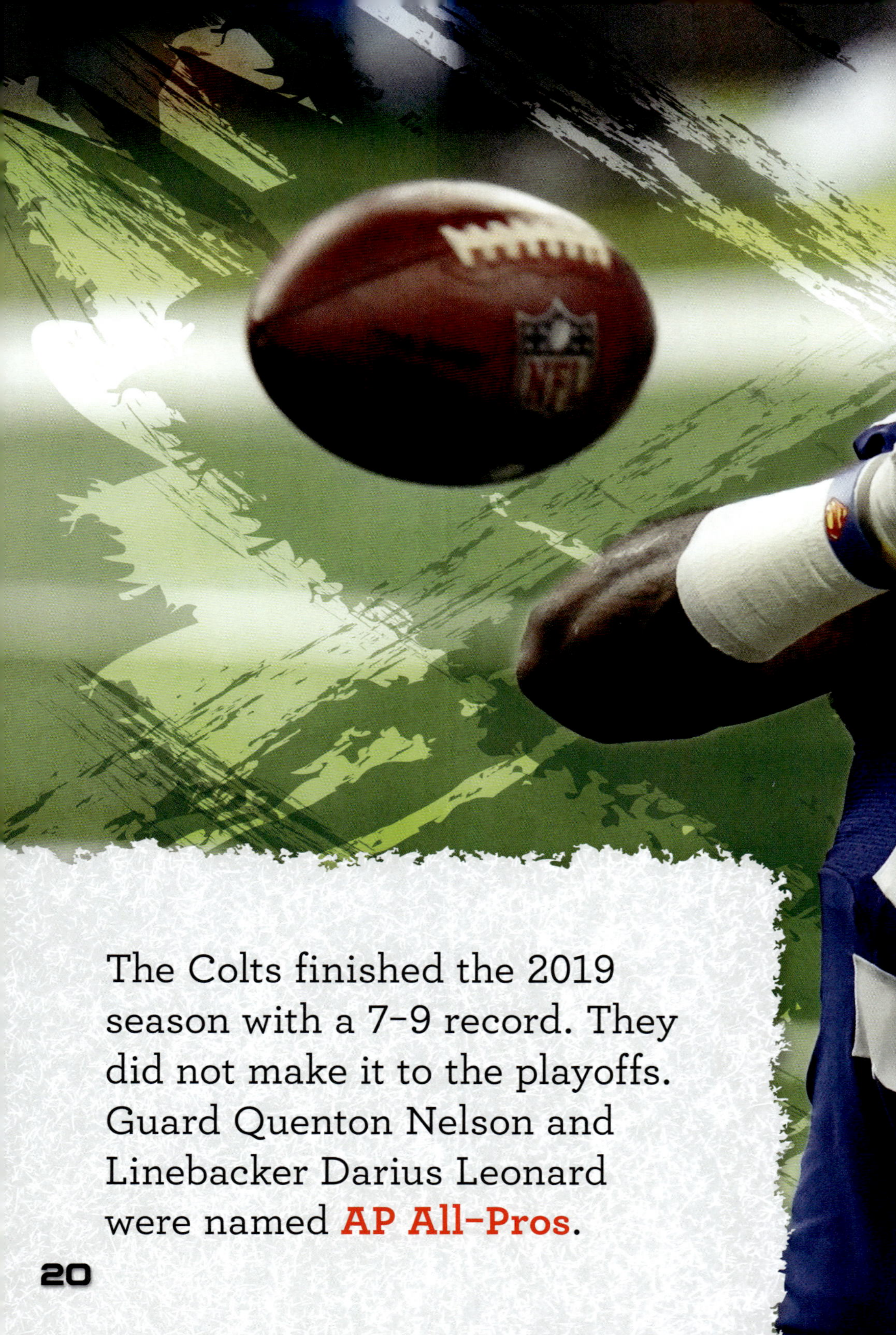

The Colts finished the 2019 season with a 7–9 record. They did not make it to the playoffs. Guard Quenton Nelson and Linebacker Darius Leonard were named **AP All-Pros**.

During the 2020 season, **quarterback** Philip Rivers joined the Colts after spending 16 years with the Chargers. He also became the fifth player on the all-time passing yards list.

HALL OF FAME

Johnny Unitas was named the NFL's Most Valuable Player (**MVP**) three times as **QB**. He threw at least one touchdown pass for 47 games in a row. That was an NFL record for more than 50 years.

Unitas played for the Colts for 17 seasons, winning two NFL **championships** and one **Super Bowl**. He was **inducted** into the Pro Football Hall of Fame in 1979.

Peyton Manning was named the league's **MVP** four times with the Colts. Manning was named the **Super Bowl's** MVP in 2007. Manning had 54,828 passing yards by the time he left team. He was **inducted** into the Pro Football Hall of Fame in 2021.

Marvin Harrison was a Colts' wide receiver for all 13 seasons of his career. He helped them win **Super Bowl** XLI and went to the **Pro Bowl** eight times! Harrison was **inducted** into the Pro Football Hall of Fame in 2016.

GLOSSARY

AP All-Pro – an honor given by press organizations to professional NFL players that names the best player at each position during a season.

championship – a game held to find a first-place winner.

induct – to admit someone as a member of an organization.

MVP – short for "most valuable player," an award given in sports to a player who has performed the best in a game or series.

Pro Bowl – a game played once a year between two teams comprised of the NFL's all-stars.

quarterback (QB) – the player on the offensive team that directs teammates in their play.

rookie – a first-year player in a professional sport.

Super Bowl – the NFL championship game, played once a year.

ONLINE RESOURCES

Booklinks
NONFICTION NETWORK
FREE! ONLINE NONFICTION RESOURCES

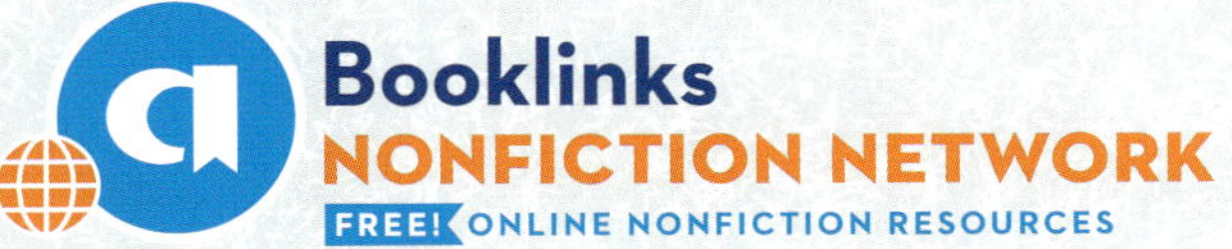

To learn more about the Indianapolis Colts, please visit **abdobooklinks.com** or scan this QR code. These links are routinely monitored and updated to provide the most current information available.

INDEX

Bears (team) 19

championships 6, 12

Chargers (team) 23

Cowboys (team) 15

Giants (team) 12

Harrison, Marvin 29

Irsay, Jim 16

Jets (team) 15

Leonard, Darius 20

Manning, Peyton 16, 26

Nelson, Quenton 20

Rivers, Philip 22

Saints (team) 19

Super Bowl 6, 15, 19

Unitas, Johnny 24, 25